The Natural History Museum

Animal Close-Ups

Monkeys

and apes and their relatives

Barbara Taylor

OXFORD

UNIVERSITY PRESS

OXFORD
UNIVERSITY PRESS

Great Clarendon Street, Oxford OX2 6DP

Oxford University Press is a department of the University of Oxford.
It furthers the University's objective of excellence in research, scholarship,
and education by publishing worldwide in

Oxford New York

Athens Auckland Bangkok Bogotá Buenos Aires
Cape Town Chennai Dar es Salaam Delhi Florence Hong Kong Istanbul
Karachi Kolkata Kuala Lumpur Madrid Melbourne Mexico City Mumbai
Nairobi Paris São Paulo Shanghai Singapore Taipei Tokyo Toronto Warsaw

with associated companies in Berlin Ibadan

Oxford is a registered trade mark of Oxford University Press
in the UK and in certain other countries

British Library Cataloguing in Publication Data available

Paperback ISBN 0 19 910790 4

1 3 5 7 9 10 8 6 4 2

Printed in Hong Kong

Contents

Orang-utan   6

Gorilla   8

Concolor gibbon   9

Bonobo   10

Chimpanzee   12

Colobus monkey   13

Guenon   14

Howler monkey   16

Spider monkey   17

Silvery marmoset   18

Golden lion tamarin   20

Black and white lemur   21

Glossary   22

Index   23

About this book
This book takes a close look at monkeys, which do
have tails, and apes, such as gorillas and chimpanzees,
which do not have tails. It will also tell you about
some rare cousins of the monkeys, such as lemurs.

I am a hairy orang-utan.

I am the largest animal that lives mainly in the trees. I live in the forests of Borneo and Sumatra in Asia.

My fingers curl into a strong grip

I am a male. I balance on the backs or sides of my half-clenched hands or feet when I walk on the ground. I can only walk upright on two legs for short distances.

I hook my long fingers over branches.

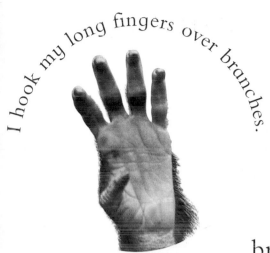

I am a young orang-utan. My strong arms are very long, which helps me to stretch from branch to branch. I have no tail.

I have a big brain, which makes me clever.

I am a giant gorilla.

I am a male silverback gorilla. I am the powerful leader of my group. I walk on all fours, resting on my tough knuckle pads.

My strong fingers are the size of bananas.

Although I may look scary, I am usually shy and gentle.

I am a swinging gibbon.

I zoom through the trees by swinging hand over hand along the branches. My long fingers grip like hooks. I can also walk upright on two legs. I do not have a tail.

I am a female. My fur became cream as I grew up.

I am a male concolor gibbon. My fur is mostly black, but my female mate has cream fur.

9

I am a gentle bonobo.

I look quite like a chimpanzee, but I am slimmer. I have a smaller head and ears, and a black face.

My big toe does not look at all like yours.

I live in a loving group of bonobos. When I was a baby, I was very close to my mother.

My thumb can touch each finger in a pincer grip.

I am clever and I can use tools and solve problems. I am also good at climbing, because my arms and legs are long and strong, and my fingers and toes grip well.

11

I am a clever chimpanzee.

I am very like you – although
I am more hairy! I cannot speak,
but I can 'talk' to other chimps
by making sounds and
pulling faces.

I am an ape. I
usually walk on
all fours, but I can
stand upright and
shuffle along on
two legs.

My bare face, big
eyes and bendy lips
help me to pull lots
of different faces.

I am a furry colobus monkey.

I come from Africa. I eat leaves and fruit and have a beautiful long cape of white hair.

I spend most of my time in the trees. I use my long tail to steer and change direction.

My hands have four fingers but no thumbs.

I have hard sitting pads on my bottom that help me to sleep sitting up.

13

I am a noisy guenon.

I come from Africa, where I live
in the trees. I have pouches
in my cheeks that help me
collect a lot of food
quickly. Then I find a
safe place to chew
and swallow it.

I have good hearing, and can pick up sounds in the forest.

I use my long fingers to grip tree branches.

My long tail helps me to balance, but it cannot grip branches.

I walk around on all fours, but I am good at leaping because my long back legs have strong muscles.

I am a heavy howler monkey.

I live in the forests of South America. I make loud howling calls that tell other howler monkeys to keep away from my patch of forest. I eat leaves and fruit.

I have wide nostrils that point to the side.

I spend most of my time in the trees. My hands, feet and tail grip tree branches firmly.

16

I am an agile spider monkey.

I am one of the largest South
American monkeys. I have
long, thin arms to help
me swing and leap
through the
trees.

My curly tail grips
the branches like
an extra hand.

My eyes help me to see a safe path through the trees.

I sometimes walk
on two legs, like
you. I use my hands
to pick fruit from
the trees.

17

I am a silvery marmoset.

I am a small monkey from South America. My body is about the same size as that of a squirrel, but my tail is much longer.

I have long, curved claws on most of my fingers and toes.

I live in a family group, with my mother, father and other silvery marmosets. I am a twin, like many marmosets.

I eat mainly fruit, but also insects, spiders and tree gum.

I am giving my baby a ride. I share carrying it with other members of my family.

I leap along branches on all fours. I am small and light, which helps me to run fast.

19

I am a playful tamarin.

I have a long mane around my face, like a lion's mane. So I am called a golden lion tamarin. I am very rare.

My long tail helps me to balance as I leap.

I use my long fingers to feel for insects under loose tree bark and in holes. My claws help me to grip branches.

I can turn my head right round to the side, to watch for danger.

I am a rare lemur.

I live only on the island of
Madagascar, off the coast
of Africa. I spend most
of my time in the
trees, and rarely come
down to the ground.

I have a very good sense of smell.

I live in a group
and help to groom
the fur of other
family members.

I run along the branches on all fours.

21

Important words

ape A clever, hairy animal with no tail. It has longer arms than legs, and grasping hands and feet.

monkey A clever, hairy animal with a tail. Its arms are not longer than its legs and it has long bendy fingers and toes.

gripping tail A tail that can wrap around and grasp objects, like an extra hand. It is called a prehensile tail.

pincer grip The way in which an ape's thumb can touch each one of its fingers, so it can grasp objects firmly.

grooming The cleaning of an animal's fur.

knuckle pads Areas of hard skin on a chimp or gorilla's knuckles.

Index

arms   7, 11, 16

ears   10, 14

eyes   17

fingers   6, 7, 8, 9, 11,
            13, 15, 18, 20

food   13, 14, 16, 17,
            19, 20

fur   9, 20, 21

grooming   21

hair   12, 13

hands   6, 9, 16, 17

legs   6, 9, 11, 13, 17

tails   7, 9, 13, 15, 16, 17

toes   10, 11, 18

trees   6, 9, 13, 16, 17, 21